Gary's Garden
Book 1

FOR BEN
Thank you for leading
me up the right garden path.

Gary's Garden: Book 1
is a
DAVID FICKLING BOOK

First published in Great Britain in 2014 by
David Fickling Books,
31 Beaumont Street,
Oxford, OX1 2NP

Text and Illustrations © Gary Northfield, 2014
Thanks to Lisa Murphy for helping with colouring the cover.

978-1-910200-09-4

1 3 5 7 9 10 8 6 4 2

David Fickling Books supports the Forest Stewardship Council (FSC®),
the leading international forest certification organisation. All our titles
that are printed on Greenpeace-approved FSC®-certified paper carry the FSC® logo.

FSC
www.fsc.org

MIX
Paper from
responsible sources
FSC® C015140

DAVID FICKLING BOOKS Reg. No. 8340307

A CIP catalogue record for this book is available from the British Library

Printed and bound in Great Britain by Polestar Stones.

CONTENTS

 This way for all the fun, chums!

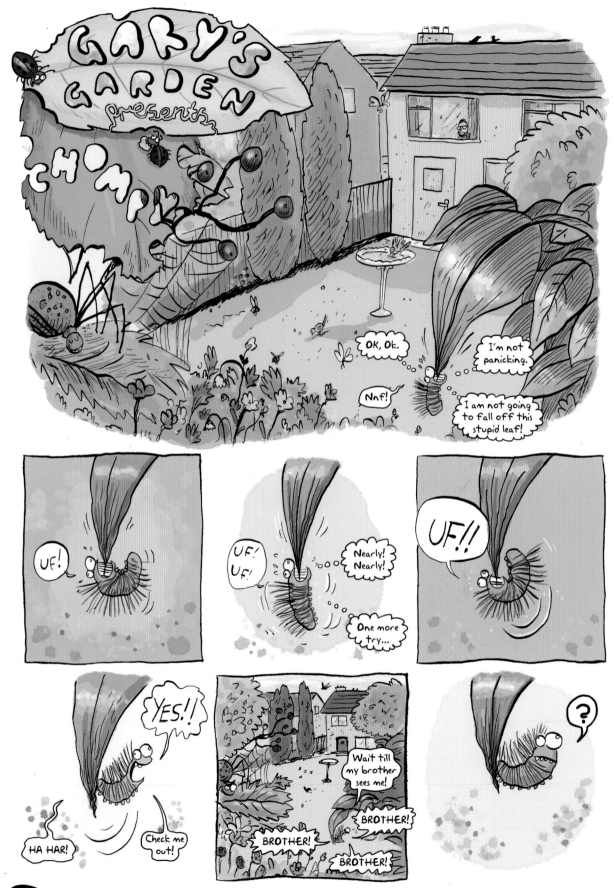

BROTHER! BROTHER! BROTHER!

Yes, yes. I'm here. What is it?

Look, brother! I'm standing on the end of a leaf! I'm a daredevil!

Bah. I haven't got time for this.

Try not to fall off and kill yourself, we're having dinner soon.

Ha! Falling off is for losers!

I'm a DAREDEVIL!

Hello?

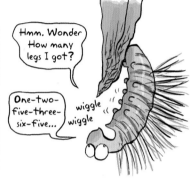

Hmm. Wonder How many legs I got?

One-two-five-three-six-five...

wiggle wiggle

Oop.

PLATCH!

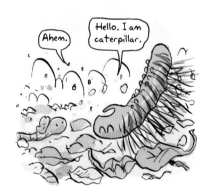

Ahem.

Hello. I am caterpillar.

Me too!

Gasp!

NO! YOU NOT Caterpillar!!

JUMP!

YOU WORM!

But we both wiggles, right?

We're the same!

NO!!

NOT THE SAME !!!!

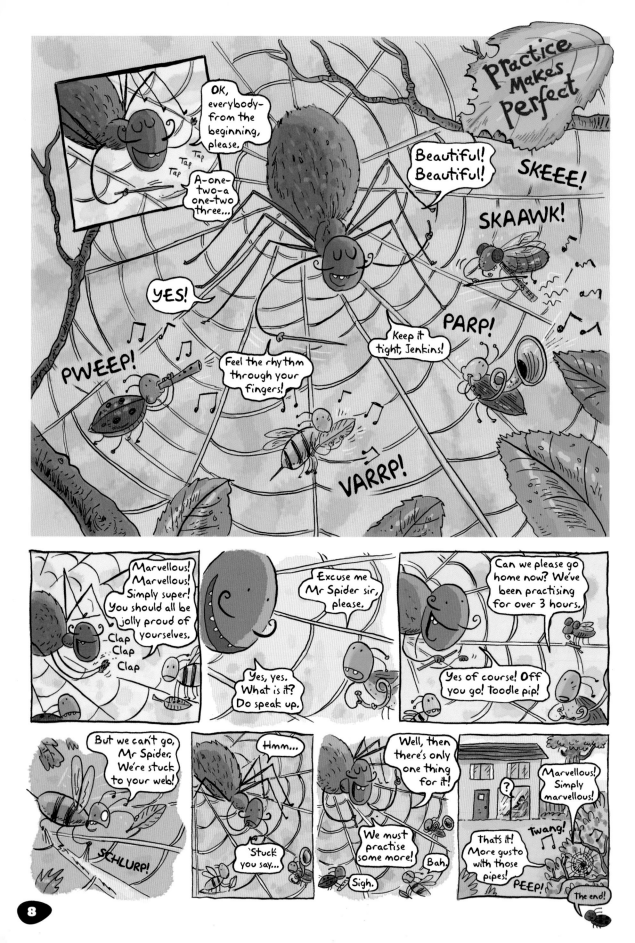

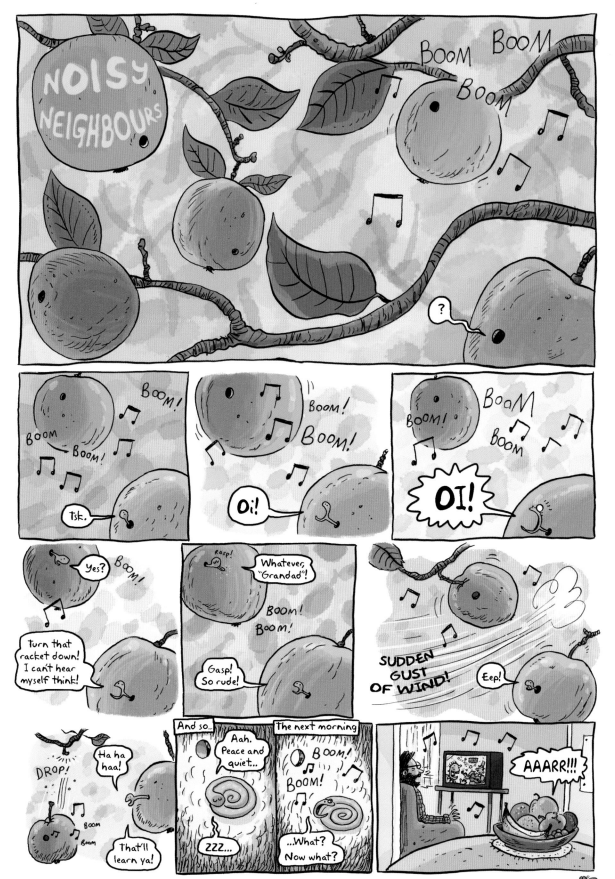

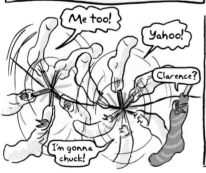

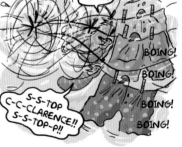

TWEEP! TWEET! CHEEP!

Yawn!

Ah...!
What a beautiful morning!

EEP!

ACORN ANTICS

All the acorns have fallen on the lawn!

That's my dinner for the next 3 months! Any flippin' idiot can get their paws on them now!

Morning, Rupert! Beautiful day, wouldn't you say?

Gotta get 'em quick!

Yeah, yeah, really lovely...

Oh my acorns, my lovely acorns... How many have I lost already? 10? 20? No time to waste!

Ooh! What's one of these?

Get your feet off, fuzzy face!

FLICK!

All right! All right!

I was only looking!

Quick! Quick! Quick!

Gotta hide 'em! Gotta hide 'em!

In my tree hole! Stuff 'em in my tree hole!

Ha har! Perfect!

I'll not lose 'em now!

Yeah, what are you looking at you idiot?

What?! You're the idiot jammed in a room full of nuts!

Such a rude squirrel...

Yeah, what do you know? You're not even a lady!

That stupid ladybird does have a point though. I can't sit like this all winter.

That night.

HA HA! Why didn't I think of it before?

I'll bury them in the dead of night.

No one will know where they are except me!!

KLANG!

I've been rumbled!

Klang! klang!

KLANK!

Jeepers! Why doesn't he shut up! The buffoon will wake up the whole garden!

They'll all see where I've buried my nuts!

3 hours later

Ho ho! Mission accomplished!

Time for some shuteye methinks!

And!

Aah! What a beautiful morning!

Time for some breakfast, I'd say!

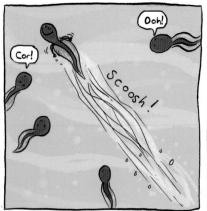

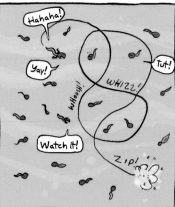

The End!

21

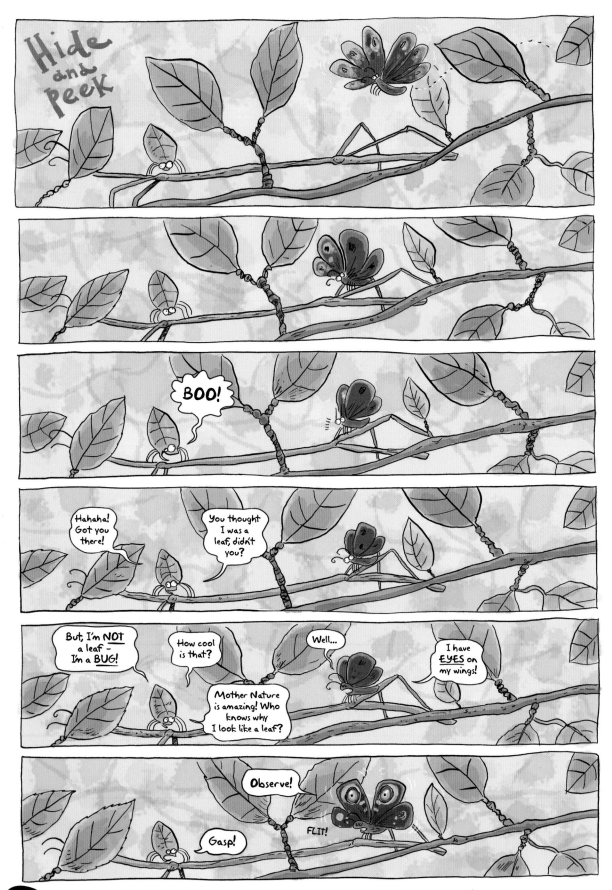

Podgy Pigeon

Man, all those breadcrumbs and we can't even eat 'em!

It's a proper crime, it is.

And all because the stupid next-door cat is sitting there, waiting for us...

Cats should be banned.

Yeah, sitting around all day eating and sleeping.

Don't sound too bad to me!

Cats eat birds, you idiot.

Oh, yeah.

Omigosh! Podgy! Podgy the pigeon is going for the bread!

?

PODGY!

PODGY!

She hasn't seen the cat!!

She's cat food for certain!

! ?

Podgy! Podgy!

There's a cat, Podgy! Scarper, quick!

Phew!

She heard just in time!

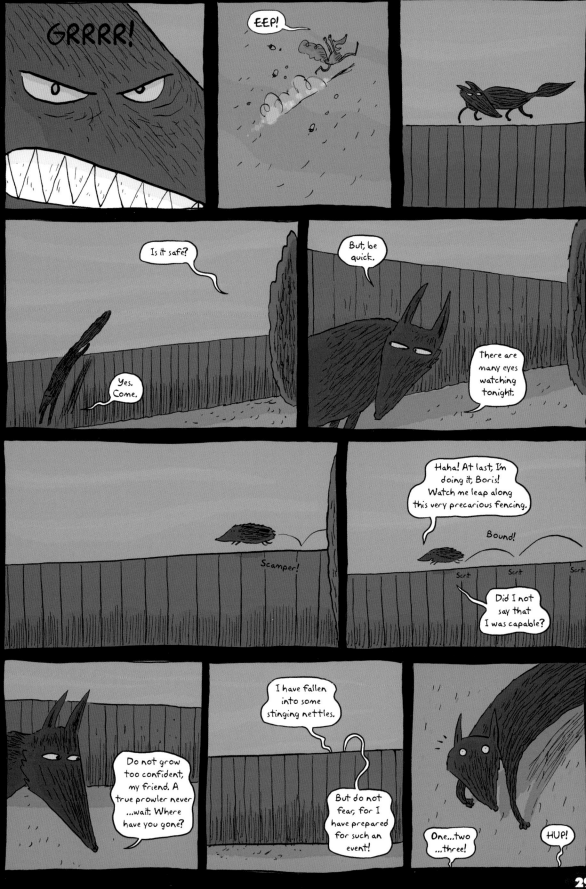

Clang!

Hup.

Hup.

Hup.

HUP!

Uh oh.

clang!

SPANG!

CLANG!

EEK!

CRASH!

MONROE!

Do not fear, Boris...

click

For, I have prepared many times for such an event.

Aw, man... How did the bin get tipped over...?

A fox!

I should've guessed! Go on! Shoo! Go eat the neighbours' rubbish, you pest!

Just look at this mess! Bleurgh!

So gross!

Stupid fox!

SLAM!

Hup!

I guess I still have much to learn...

Yes. One has to work very hard not to be seen in these situations.

Ah, but Boris, was it the hedgehog or the fox who was seen tonight?

You tell me!

The End!

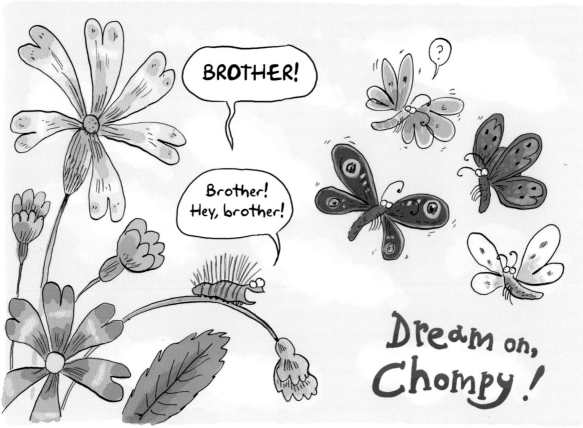

Dream on, Chompy!

The End!

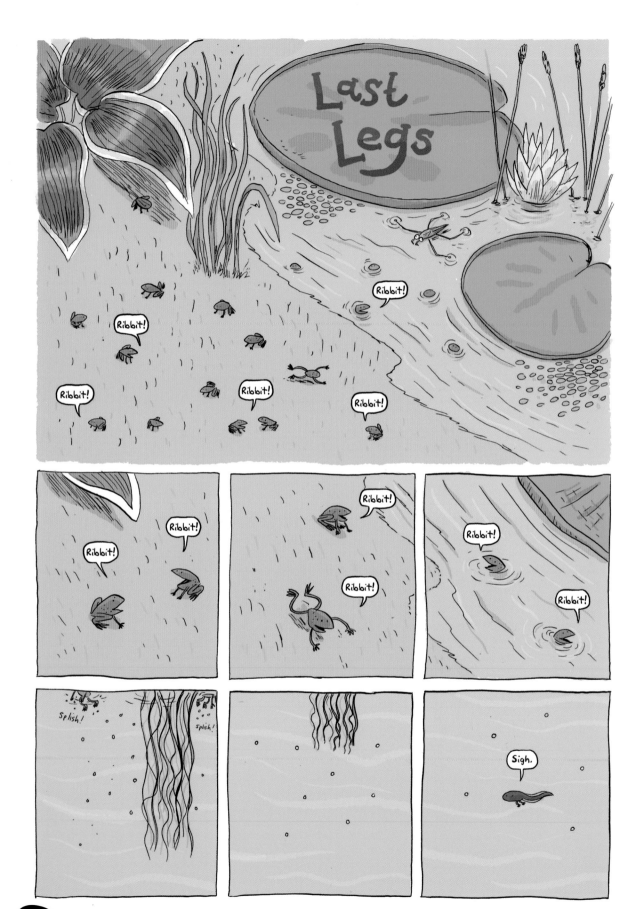

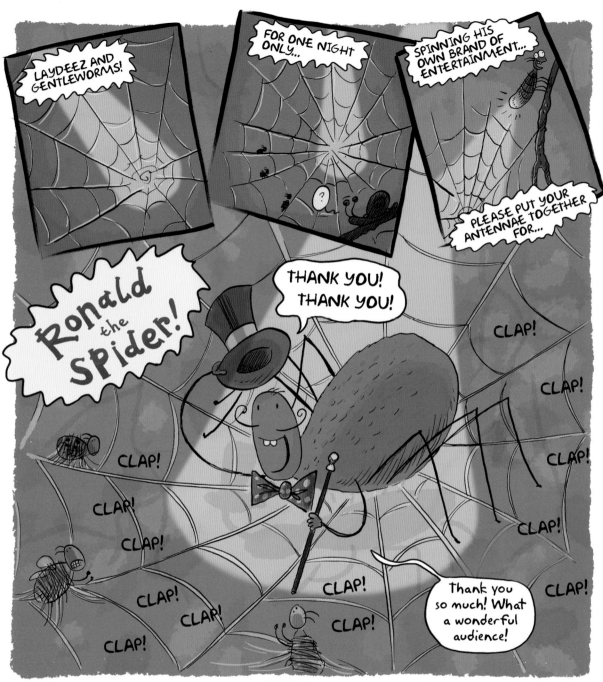

Zarpovia!
part 1

Trundle!
Trundle!

KLONK!

We have arrived!

ARR!

Egads!

Quickly! Through the dimensional gateway!

We must hurry, for once it closes, we'll be forever trapped in another universe!

Straight ahead! Run! Run!

Be wary! Danger hides around every corner. Spiders the size of sunflowers!

Is this the alien world that you observed, professor?

It's like nothing I have ever witnessed!

No! This is not the world! Shield your eyes! Peering into this dimension for more than a minute will reduce you to babbling buffoons! Come away!

At last!

Behold! The alien world that I have named, "Zarpovia"!

Gasp!

Ooh!

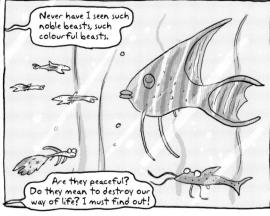

Never have I seen such noble beasts, such colourful beasts.

Are they peaceful? Do they mean to destroy our way of life? I must find out!

Way ahead of you, professor! I shall climb this cliff face with one bound!

Leap!

Wait, John! Something stirs up there! Perhaps a monster!

Gragh!

I see him, professor.

The eight-legged fiend doesn't frighten me!

Have at ye!

Ragh!

But!

AAIEE!

RAAGH!

JOHN!

Is this the end for John Ladybird? Will our heroes discover the secrets of Zarpovia? Tune in again for another exciting episode of GARY'S GARDEN!

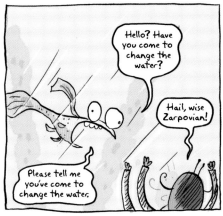

47

Camouflage Club

You ain't seen me.

Good afternoon, everyone!

I'd like to thank you all for coming along to this month's Camouflage Club!

My name is Lydia Leaf Bug and this is Sticky the Stick Insect.

I'm over here.

...Who is over here.

Wait a minute...

Is anyone else actually here at this camouflage meeting?

Yup,

Yep,

Right here.

Yes,

Right, phew! Okaay. Onto our first item on the agenda: new members.

Bzzz

Ooh, hello! Is this the Camouflage Club?

Um, yes.

Great! Can I join please?

The End!

49

Nice Hat

What's Whatsisface doing?

Why is he just sitting there?

Why isn't he putting the crusts out? I'm starving!

You're always starving.

Whatever.

WHERE'S OUR CRUSTS, CRUSTY?

HA HA HA!

From the look of it, he's scoffed them all himself!

Slurp!

All right, chaps?

Have you seen his new hat?

Totally!

Ha ha!

He'll never get a girlfriend wearing that stupid thing!

PICK!

Here, watch this.

"Hello ladies, do you like my new hat?"

Ha Ha Ha

What was THAT?

That's an impression of Whatsisface wearing his new hat!

That's terrible!

Nothing like him!

Yo! What's up, dudes?

Clarence!

Clarence does a good impression of Whatsisface. Come on Clarence, show us!

Nah, not today. It's not that good.

Go on, Clarence! It's a bit like this, "Cooee! Who wants some cake? I do!"

Ha! That's not it!

You do it then!

Oh please, Clarence! Please do your impression.

Oh, go on then.

Ahem... ready?

Yes!

"Hello! Look at me! I've got a big stupid beard!"

Ha Ha Ha Ha Ha Ha! Ha

Ha

Ha

Tweet! Tweet! Tweet! Tweet! Tweet!

Aah! I could sit here and listen to those birds tweeting all day!

the End!

51

Grumpy Spiders

Mimicry Club

Welcome one and all to this month's MIMICRY CLUB!

Flap!

I'm Bobby Butterfly – I have spots on my wings that mimic eyes!

And this is Anton. Anton is a hover fly who looks like a wasp!

How do.

AAIIEE!!!

A WASP!

Who let one of those in here?!

Run for your lives!

?

WAIT! WAIT! I'M NOT A WASP, I JUST LOOK LIKE A WASP!

Oh right!

Phew! I did wonder.

That was close!

OK, everyone settle down. I think we should start by everyone introducing themselves and saying a little bit about their mimicry.

How about you first, Mr Spider?

Who me?

Um... ok... My name's Rodney and I'm a Zebra Jumping Spider.

Hello Rodney and welcome to the club.

And what is it that you mimic?

Um...a zebra, I guess.

Oh, er...right. I'm not actually sure that you actually do. But it doesn't matter! Let's move on to the next one...

But I want to be a dinosaur too!

Please!

No! I'm always a dinosaur!

You'll have to pretend to be something else.

Otherwise you can't join our gang.

Well, maybe I don't want to join your stupid gang!

?

Hey, guys! Check it out!

This leaf's got a face!

What?

Where?

Here, look!

He's got a pair of eyes!

That has got to be the stupidest thing I've ever heard!

How can a leaf have a face?

You really are ridiculous sometimes.

Don't worry, I love you, Mr Leaf.

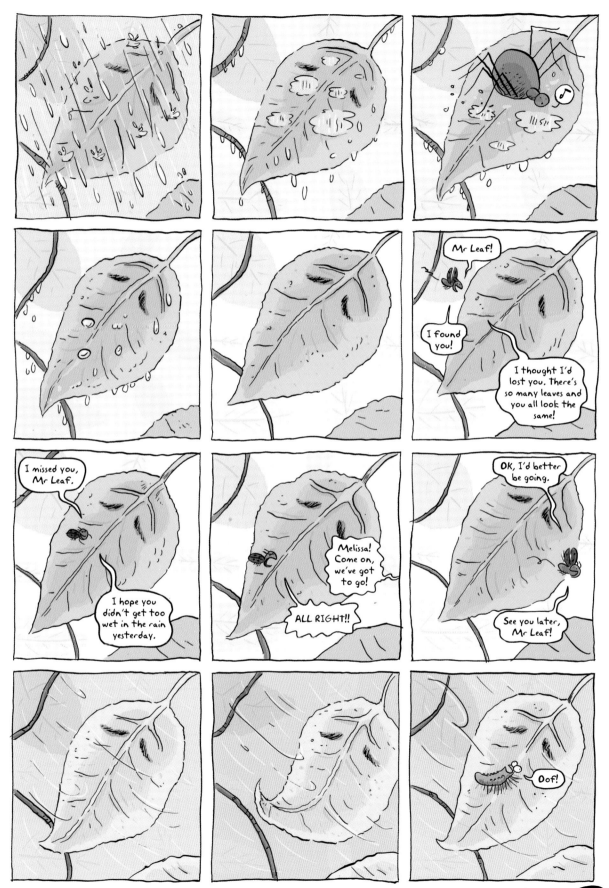

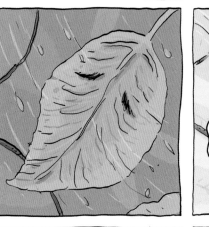

Gary's Garden

TOP CHUMPS

WHO HAS THE MOST LEGS? WHO IS THE ICKIEST IN THE GARDEN? WHO IS THE WORLD'S WORST ROTTER AND WHO IS THE TOP CHUMP? GET THE LOWDOWN ON YOUR GARY'S GARDEN FAVOURITES WITH THESE HANDY SCORE CARDS! DOWNLOAD THE CARDS FROM: WWW.THEPHOENIXCOMIC.CO.UK/TOPCHUMPS

CHOMPY

Intelligence	2
Heroism	4
Grumpiness	9
Ickiness	8
Legs	16

Grumpy caterpillar, forever annoying his butterfly brother, Bert. Quite enjoys rollicking adventures with mad ladybirds.

RUPERT

Intelligence	6
Heroism	5
Grumpiness	7
Ickiness	2
Legs	2

Skittish nut job. Do NOT nick his acorns. Or even LOOK at his acorns. In fact forget I even mentioned his stupid acorns.

WIGGLES

Intelligence	2
Heroism	2
Grumpiness	1
Ickiness	10
Legs	0

The happiest caterpillar in the garden. Loves that her best friend is ANOTHER caterpillar. Yay! Wiggles and Chompy BFF!

JENNIFER

Intelligence	6
Heroism	3
Grumpiness	9
Ickiness	9
Legs	Just the 2

Should be a frog, but isn't a frog. Should have four legs, but only has two. Life was much more fun when no one had any legs.

DAPHNE

'Scuse me! 'Scuse me!

Intelligence	3
Heroism	7
Grumpiness	2
Ickiness	6
Legs	2

Loves twigs and art and can do a pretty mean elephant impression. Would join more clubs if only there were enough hours in the day.

MONROE

Intelligence	7
Heroism	10
Grumpiness	1
Ickiness	2
Legs	4

Apprentice night-time ninja. Eager to please his master, Boris, and thinks he's ready to go it alone. Boris has different ideas...

CHRIS

Intelligence	8
Heroism	7
Grumpiness	10
Ickiness	9
Legs	8

Big, grumpy spider. Try not to fly into his web, especially when he's in the middle of an argument with the annoying spider next door.

PROF. ZARPOV

Intelligence	10
Heroism	9
Grumpiness	4
Ickiness	7
Legs	6

At the forefront of ladybird science. Explorer of inter-dimensional worlds using hi-tech contraptions of his own invention.

LYDIA

Intelligence	8
Heroism	7
Grumpiness	1
Ickiness	9
Legs	6

Looking like a leaf is probably the greatest thing to happen to Lydia. Her best friend is a stick insect who looks like a twig! Would now like a friend who looks like a flower.

RONALD

Intelligence	9
Heroism	4
Grumpiness	1
Ickiness	9
Legs	8

Ronald loves to entertain and is always on the lookout for a captive audience for his brilliant new jokes and dance moves.

PENNY

Intelligence	6
Heroism	4
Grumpiness	4
Ickiness	7
Legs	2

Frequent visitor to the garden, but doesn't interact much with the others, especially as it diverts attention from any crusts that have to be eaten.

STICKY

Intelligence	9
Heroism	5
Grumpiness	6
Ickiness	10
Legs	6

Lives next door but prefers the company of Gary's Garden. Although everyone gets on his nerves there too, to be frank.

BORIS

Intelligence	9
Heroism	10
Grumpiness	6
Ickiness	3
Legs	4

Expert night-time ninja. Has taken promising hedgehog Monroe under his wing. Can barely cope with his cheekiness, let alone much else.

HARRIET

Intelligence	7
Heroism	7
Grumpiness	4
Ickiness	2
Legs	2

Sociable little bird who appreciates having a little gang to hang around with. Wishes there was more than just breadcrumbs to eat, though.

BRIAN

Intelligence	8
Heroism	1
Grumpiness	9
Ickiness	10
Legs	4

They don't come nastier, stinkier, or, er, rottener, than night-time villain Brian the rat. Quite likes a bag of chips for dinner.

LARRY

Intelligence	5
Heroism	10
Grumpiness	3
Ickiness	7
Legs	6

Lord of the jungle! Few are those that match his courage and taste for adventure. Even understands a little of the Ancient Ladybird language.

TERRENCE

Intelligence	7
Heroism	8
Grumpiness	8
Ickiness	9
Legs	1

Terrence just wants to go on mad adventures stealing food and disappearing off into strange distant lands. WHY DOESN'T HIS MUM UNDERSTAND?!

CLARENCE

Intelligence	7
Heroism	9
Scarcity	3
Ickiness	2
Legs	2

Happy-go-lucky Great Tit. Loves noodles, big underpants, and can do an amazing impression of 'Whatsisface'.

GARY

Intelligence	10
Heroism	10
Grumpiness	10
Ickiness	10
Legs	10

Oblivious owner of the garden. Loves all the little birdies and creepy crawlies, but is not certain if that love is returned. (It's not.)

SANDRA

Well, this is awkward.

Intelligence	7
Heroism	5
Grumpiness	3
Ickiness	6
Legs	4

Loves to dress up at every occasion. Past costumes include a hedgehog, a bag of chips, a rock and Troy Trailblazer.

ANTON

Intelligence	6
Heroism	5
Grumpiness	7
Ickiness	8
Legs	6

Hoverfly Anton keeps being told he looks like a wasp. Wishes he just looked like a hoverfly and everyone would shut up.

MR LEAF

Intelligence	0
Heroism	0
Grumpiness	9
Ickiness	0
Legs	0

A leaf with a face on it. Looks very old and wise, but probably isn't. Now serves as a blanket for ninja hedgehog, Monroe.

BOBBY

Intelligence	7
Heroism	5
Grumpiness	8
Ickiness	3
Legs	6

Butterfly with impressive eyes on his wings. Not that he can see with them or anything. Don't mention Camouflage Club.

JOHN

Intelligence	8
Heroism	10
Grumpiness	4
Ickiness	6
Legs	6

Inter-dimensional traveller. Has visited Mars, Zarpovia and the distant future. Is very excited about his upcoming holiday to Clacton.

BENNY

Intelligence	7
Heroism	3
Grumpiness	8
Ickiness	10
Legs	0

Weird being from Zarpovia, a new universe within a universe inside Gary's house. Chompy thinks it's a Guppy, but what does he know?

TRISH

Intelligence	8
Heroism	4
Grumpiness	10
Ickiness	10
Legs	0

Little apple worm suffering the problems of apple social housing, i.e. LOTS OF STUPID NOISY NEIGHBOURS!!!

RODNEY

Intelligence	7
Heroism	3
Grumpiness	6
Ickiness	5
Legs	8

A lover of art, Rodney would one day love to be a famous artist. Or, if that doesn't work out, a zebra impersonator.

BERT

Intelligence	7
Heroism	8
Grumpiness	9
Ickiness	3
Legs	6

Chompy's grumpy brother Bert. Is grumpy because Chompy is such a full-time idiot. How he wishes for a quiet life...

HENRY

Intelligence	8
Heroism	7
Grumpiness	3
Ickiness	6
Legs	8

Henry is very old and has seen many changes to the garden over the years. Wishes the youngsters would slow down a bit - just for a chat!

GWENDOLIN

Intelligence	8
Heroism	6
Grumpiness	1
Ickiness	2
Legs	6

It's not often you get rescued by a dashing hero in a loin-cloth, but who was he? Where did he come from? And does he want his loincloth back?

RAY

Intelligence	7
Heroism	5
Grumpiness	7
Ickiness	9
Legs	0

Ray isn't a snake - he's not even a worm. He's a SLOW WORM. Slow Worms are lizards without legs, just so you know. Not that anyone listens.

THELMA

Intelligence	9
Heroism	7
Grumpiness	1
Ickiness	4
Legs	4

Thelma has a good nose for food, so long as it's vegetarian. She does like worms, mind it's just that she couldn't eat a whole one.

HUMPHREY

Intelligence	8
Heroism	9
Grumpiness	2
Ickiness	9
Legs	6

Being a blue bottle means having your wits about you at all times. Fortunately, spiders are a bit stupid, so most nasty encounters are easily avoided. Just.

MELISSA

Intelligence	8
Heroism	8
Grumpiness	4
Ickiness	3
Legs	6

Her best friend is Mr Leaf. He's the only one who listens to Melissa and her troubles. She hopes Mr Leaf appreciates the drawing she did of him!